THE SPIRIT OF TERRORISM

and

Other Essays

◆

JEAN BAUDRILLARD

Translated by Chris Turner

VERSO

London • New York

First published by Verso 2002
© Verso 2002
Translation © Chris Turner 2002
This edition first published by Verso 2003
© Verso 2003
Translation © Chris Turner 2003
The Spirit of Terrorism first published as
L'esprit du terrorisme © Éditions Galilée 2002
Requiem for the Twin Towers first published as
Requiem pour les Twin Towers © Jean Baudrillard 2002
Hypotheses on Terrorism first published as
Hypothèses sur le terrorisme © Éditions Galilée 2002
The Violence of the Global first published as
La violence du mondial © Éditions Galilée 2002
All rights reserved

7 9 10 8

Verso
UK: 6 Meard Street, London W1F 0EG
USA: 20 Jay Street, Suite 1010, Brooklyn, NY 11201
www.versobooks.com

Verso is the imprint of New Left Books

ISBN-13: 978-1-85984-448-9

British Library Cataloguing in Publication Data
A catalogue record for this book is available from the British Library

Library of Congress Cataloging-in-Publication Data
A catalog record for this book is available from the
Library of Congress

Typeset in Perpetua by M Rules
Printed in the USA by Maple Vail

CONTENTS

THE SPIRIT OF
TERRORISM

When it comes to world events, we had seen quite a few. From the death of Diana to the World Cup. And violent, real events, from wars right through to genocides. Yet, when it comes to symbolic events on a world scale – that is to say not just events that gain worldwide coverage, but events that represent a setback for globalization itself – we had had none. Throughout the stagnation of the 1990s, events were 'on strike' (as the Argentinian writer Macedonio Fernandez put it). Well, the strike is over now. Events are not on strike any more. With the attacks on the World

Trade Center in New York, we might even be said to have before us the absolute event, the 'mother' of all events, the pure event uniting within itself all the events that have never taken place.

The whole play of history and power is disrupted by this event, but so, too, are the conditions of analysis. You have to take your time. While events were stagnating, you had to anticipate and move more quickly than they did. But when they speed up this much, you have to move more slowly – though without allowing yourself to be buried beneath a welter of words, or the gathering clouds of war, and preserving intact the unforgettable incandescence of the images.

All that has been said and written is evidence of a gigantic abreaction to the event itself, and the fascination it exerts. The moral condemnation and the holy alliance against terrorism are on the same scale as the prodigious jubilation at seeing this global superpower destroyed – better, at seeing it, in a sense, destroying itself, committing suicide in a blaze of glory. For it is that superpower which, by its unbearable power, has fomented all this violence which is endemic throughout the world, and hence that (unwittingly) terroristic imagination which dwells in all of us.

The fact that we have dreamt of this event, that everyone without exception has dreamt of it – because no one can avoid dreaming of the destruction of any power that has become hegemonic to this degree – is unacceptable to the Western moral conscience. Yet it is a fact, and one which can indeed be measured by the emotive violence of all that has been said and written in the effort to dispel it.

At a pinch, we can say that they *did it*, but we *wished for* it. If this is not taken into account, the event loses any symbolic dimension. It becomes a pure accident, a purely arbitrary act, the murderous phantasmagoria of a few fanatics, and all that would then remain would be to eliminate them. Now, we know very well that this is not how it is.

Which explains all the counterphobic ravings about exorcizing evil: it is because it is there, everywhere, like an obscure object of desire. Without this deep-seated complicity, the event would not have had the resonance it has, and in their symbolic strategy the terrorists doubtless know that they can count on this unavowable complicity.

This goes far beyond hatred for the dominant world power among the disinherited and the exploited, among those who have ended up on the wrong side of the global order. Even those who share in the advantages of that order have this malicious desire in their hearts. Allergy to any definitive order, to any definitive power, is – happily – universal, and the two towers of the World Trade Center were perfect embodiments, in their very twinness, of that definitive order.

No need, then, for a death drive or a destructive instinct, or even for perverse, unintended effects. Very logically – and inexorably – the increase in the power of power heightens the will to destroy it. And it was party to its own destruction. When the two towers collapsed, you had the impression that they were responding to the suicide of the suicide-planes with their own suicides. It has been said that 'Even God cannot declare war on Himself.' Well, He can. The West, in the position of God (divine omnipotence and absolute moral legitimacy), has become suicidal, and declared war on itself.

The countless disaster movies bear witness to this fantasy, which they clearly attempt to exorcize with images, drowning out the whole thing with special effects. But the universal attraction they exert, which is on a par with pornography, shows that acting-out is never very far away, the impulse to reject any system growing all the stronger as it approaches perfection or omnipotence.

It is probable that the terrorists had not foreseen the collapse of the Twin Towers (any more than had the experts!), a collapse which — much more than the attack on the Pentagon – had the greatest symbolic impact. The symbolic collapse of a whole system came about by an unpredictable complicity, as though the towers, by collapsing on their own, by committing suicide, had joined in to round off the event. In a sense, the entire system, by its internal fragility, lent the initial action a helping hand.

The more concentrated the system becomes globally, ultimately forming one single network, the more it becomes vulnerable at a single point (already a single little Filipino hacker had managed, from the dark recesses of his portable computer, to launch the 'I love you' virus, which circled the globe devastating entire networks). Here it was eighteen suicide attackers who, thanks to the absolute weapon of death, enhanced by technological efficiency, unleashed a global catastrophic process.

When global power monopolizes the situation to this extent, when there is such a formidable condensation of all functions in the technocratic machinery, and when no alternative form of thinking is allowed, what other way is there but a *terroristic situational transfer*? It was the system itself which created the objective conditions for this brutal retaliation. By seizing all the cards for itself, it forced the Other to change the rules. And the new rules are fierce ones, because the stakes are fierce. To a system whose very excess of power poses an insoluble challenge, the terrorists respond with a definitive act which is also not susceptible of exchange. Terrorism is the act that restores an irreducible singularity to the heart of a system of generalized exchange. All the singularities (species, individuals and cultures) that have paid with their deaths for the installation of a global circulation governed by a single power are taking their revenge today through this *terroristic situational transfer*.

This is terror against terror – there is no longer any ideology behind it. We are far beyond ideology and politics now. No ideology, no cause – not even the Islamic cause – can account for the energy which fuels terror. The aim is no longer even to transform the world, but (as the heresies did in their day) to radicalize the world by sacrifice. Whereas the system aims to realize it by force.

Terrorism, like viruses, is everywhere. There is a global perfusion of terrorism, which accompanies any system of domination as though it were its shadow, ready to activate itself anywhere, like a double agent. We can no longer draw a demarcation line around it. It is at the very heart of this culture which combats it, and the visible fracture (and the hatred) that pits the exploited and the underdeveloped globally against the Western world secretly connects with the fracture internal to the dominant system. That system can face down any visible antagonism. But against the other kind, which is viral in structure – as though every machinery of domination secreted its own counterapparatus, the agent of its own disappearance – against that form of almost automatic reversion of its own power, the system can do nothing. And terrorism is the shock wave of this silent reversion.

This is not, then, a clash of civilizations or religions, and it reaches far beyond Islam and America, on which efforts are being made to focus the conflict in order to create the delusion of a visible confrontation and a solution based on force. There is, indeed, a fundamental antagonism here, but one which points past the spectre of America (which is, perhaps, the epicentre, but in no sense the sole embodiment, of globalization) and the spectre of Islam (which is not the embodiment of terrorism either), to *triumphant globaliza tion battling against itself*. In this sense, we can indeed speak of a world war — not the Third World War, but the Fourth and the only really global one, since what is at stake is globalization itself. The first two world wars corresponded to the classical image of war. The first ended the supremacy of Europe and the colonial era. The second put an end to Nazism. The third, which has indeed taken place, in the form of cold war and deterrence, put an end to Communism. With each succeeding war, we have moved further towards a single world order. Today that order, which has virtually reached its culmination, finds itself grappling with the antagonistic forces scattered throughout the very heartlands of the global, in all the current convulsions. A fractal war of all cells, all singularities, revolting in the form of antibodies. A confrontation so impossible to pin down that the idea of war has to be rescued from time to time by spectacular set-pieces, such as the Gulf War or the war in Afghanistan. But the Fourth World War is elsewhere. It is what haunts every world order, all hegemonic domination – if Islam dominated the world, terrorism would rise against Islam, *for it is the world, the globe itself, which resists globalization.*

Terrorism is immoral. The World Trade Center event, that symbolic challenge, is immoral, and it is a response to a globalization which is itself immoral. So, let us be immoral; and if we want to have some understanding of all this, let us go and take a little look beyond Good and Evil. When, for once, we have an event that defies not just morality, but any form of interpretation, let us try to approach it with an understanding of Evil.

This is precisely where the crucial point lies — in the total misunderstanding on the part of Western philosophy, on the part of the Enlightenment, of the relation between Good and Evil. We believe naively that the progress of Good, its advance in all fields (the sciences, technology, democracy, human rights), corresponds to a defeat of Evil. No one seems to have understood that Good and Evil advance together, as part of the same movement. The triumph of the one does not eclipse the other — far from it. In metaphysical terms, Evil is regarded as an accidental mishap, but this axiom, from which all the Manichaean forms of the struggle of Good against Evil derive, is illusory. Good does not conquer Evil, nor indeed does the reverse happen: they are at once both irreducible to each other and inextricably interrelated. Ultimately, Good could thwart Evil only by ceasing to be Good since, by seizing for itself a global monopoly of power, it gives rise, by that very act, to a blowback of a proportionate violence.

In the traditional universe, there was still a balance between Good and Evil, in accordance with a dialectical relation which maintained the tension and equilibrium of the moral universe, come what may – not unlike the way the confrontation of the two powers in the Cold War maintained the balance of terror. There was, then, no supremacy of the one over the other. As soon as there was a total extrapolation of Good (hegemony of the positive over any form of negativity, exclusion of death and of any potential adverse force – triumph of the values of Good all along the line), that balance was upset. From this point on, the equilibrium was gone, and it was as though Evil regained an invisible autonomy, henceforward developing exponentially.

Relatively speaking, this is more or less what has happened in the political order with the eclipse of Communism and the global triumph of liberal power: it was at that point that a ghostly enemy emerged, infiltrating itself throughout the whole planet, slipping in everywhere like a virus, welling up from all the interstices of power: Islam. But Islam was merely the moving front along which the antagonism crystallized. The antagonism is everywhere, and in every one of us. So, it is terror against terror. But asymmetric terror. And it is this asymmetry which leaves global omnipotence entirely disarmed. At odds with itself, it can only plunge further into its own logic of relations of force, but it cannot operate on the terrain of the symbolic challenge and death – a thing of which it no longer has any idea, since it has erased it from its own culture.

Up to the present, this integrative power has largely succeeded in absorbing and resolving any crisis, any negativity, creating, as it did so, a situation of the deepest despair (not only for the disinherited, but for the pampered and privileged too, in their radical comfort). The fundamental change now is that the terrorists have ceased to commit suicide for no return; they are now bringing their own deaths to bear in an effective, offensive manner, in the service of an intuitive strategic insight which is quite simply a sense of the immense fragility of the opponent – a sense that a system which has arrived at its quasi-perfection can, by that very token, be ignited by the slightest spark. They have succeeded in turning their own deaths into an absolute weapon against a system that operates on the basis of the exclusion of death, a system whose ideal is an ideal of zero deaths. Every zero-death system is a zero-sum-game system. And all the means of deterrence and destruction can do nothing against an enemy who has already turned his death into a counterstrike weapon. 'What does the American bombing matter? Our men are as eager to die as the Americans are to live!' Hence the non-equivalence of the four thousand deaths inflicted at a stroke on a zero-death system.

Here, then, it is all about death, not only about the violent irruption of death in real time –

'live', so to speak – but the irruption of a death which is far more than real: a death which is symbolic and sacrificial – that is to say, the absolute, irrevocable event.

This is the spirit of terrorism.

Never attack the system in terms of relations of force. That is the (revolutionary) imagination the system itself forces upon you – the system which survives only by constantly drawing those attacking it into fighting on the ground of reality, which is always its own. But shift the struggle into the symbolic sphere, where the rule is that of challenge, reversion and outbidding. *So that death can be met only by equal or greater death.* Defy the system by a gift to which it cannot respond except by its own death and its own collapse.

The terrorist hypothesis is that the system itself will commit suicide in response to the multiple challenges posed by deaths and suicides.

For there is a symbolic obligation upon both the system and power [*le pouvoir*], and in this trap lies the only chance of their catastrophic collapse. In this vertiginous cycle of the impossible exchange of death, the death of the terrorist is an infinitesimal point, but one that creates a gigantic suction or void, an enormous convection. Around this tiny point the whole system of the real and of power [*la puissance*] gathers, transfixed; rallies briefly; then perishes by its own hyperefficiency.

It is the tactic of the terrorist model to bring about an excess of reality, and have the system collapse beneath that excess of reality. The whole derisory nature of the situation, together with the violence mobilized by the system, turns around against it, for terrorist acts are both the exorbitant mirror of its own violence and the model of a symbolic violence forbidden to it, the only violence it cannot exert – that of its own death.

This is why the whole of visible power can do

nothing against the tiny, but symbolic, death of a few individuals.

We have to face facts, and accept that a new terrorism has come into being, a new form of action which plays the game, and lays hold of the rules of the game, solely with the aim of disrupting it. Not only do these people not play fair, since they put their own deaths into play – to which there is no possible response ('they are cowards') – but they have taken over all the weapons of the dominant power. Money and stock-market speculation, computer technology and aeronautics, spectacle and the media networks – they have assimilated everything of modernity and globalism, without changing their goal, which is to destroy that power.

They have even – and this is the height of cunning – used the banality of American everyday life as cover and camouflage. Sleeping in their suburbs, reading and studying with their families, before activating themselves suddenly like time bombs. The faultless mastery of this clandestine style of operation is almost as terroristic as the spectacular act of September 11, since it casts suspicion on any and every individual. Might not any inoffensive person be a potential terrorist? If *they* could pass unnoticed, then each of us is a criminal going unnoticed (every plane also becomes suspect), and in the end, this is no doubt true. This may very well correspond to an unconscious form of potential, veiled, carefully repressed criminality, which is always capable, if not of resurfacing, at least of thrilling secretly to the spectacle of Evil. So the event ramifies down to the smallest detail – the source of an even more subtle mental terrorism.

The radical difference is that the terrorists, while they have at their disposal weapons that are the system's own, possess a further lethal weapon: their own deaths. If they were content just to fight the system with its own weapons, they would immediately be eliminated. If they merely used their own deaths to combat it, they would disappear just as quickly in a useless sacrifice — as terrorism has almost always done up to now (an example being the Palestinian suicide attacks), for which reason it has been doomed to failure.

As soon as they combine all the modern resources available to them with this highly symbolic weapon, everything changes. The destructive potential is multiplied to infinity. It is this multiplication of factors (which seem irreconcilable to us) that gives them such superiority. The 'zero-death' strategy, by contrast, the strategy of the 'clean' technological war, precisely fails to match up to this transfiguration of 'real' power by symbolic power.

The prodigious success of such an attack presents a problem, and if we are to gain some understanding of it, we have to slough off our Western perspective to see what goes on in the terrorists' organization, and in their heads. With us, such efficiency would assume a maximum of calculation and rationality that we find hard to imagine in others. And, even in this case, as in any rational organization or secret service, there would always have been leaks or slip-ups.

So, the secret of such a success lies elsewhere. The difference is that here we are dealing not with an employment contract, but with a pact and a sacrificial obligation. Such an obligation is immune to any defection or corruption. The miracle is to have adapted to the global network and technical protocols, without losing anything of this complicity 'unto death'. Unlike the contract, the pact does not bind individuals – even their 'suicide' is not individual heroism, it is a collective sacrificial act sealed by an ideal demand. And it is the combination of two mechanisms – an operational structure and a symbolic pact – that made an act of such excessiveness possible.

We no longer have any idea what a symbolic calculation is, as in poker or potlatch: with minimum stakes, but the maximum result. And the maximum result was precisely what the terrorists obtained in the Manhattan attack, which might be presented as quite a good illustration of chaos theory: an initial impact causing incalculable consequences; whereas the Americans' massive deployment ('Desert Storm') achieved only derisory effects — the hurricane ending, so to speak, in the beating of a butterfly's wing.

Suicidal terrorism was a terrorism of the poor. This is a terrorism of the rich. This is what particularly frightens us: the fact that they have become rich (they have all the necessary resources) without ceasing to wish to destroy us. Admittedly, in terms of our system of values, they are cheating. It is not playing fair to throw one's own death into the game. But this does not trouble them, and the new rules are not ours to determine.

So any argument is used to discredit their acts. For example, calling them 'suicidal' and 'martyrs' — and adding immediately that martyrdom proves nothing, that it has nothing to do with truth, that it is even (to quote Nietzsche) the enemy number one of truth. Admittedly, their deaths prove nothing, but in a system where truth itself is elusive (or do we claim to possess it?), there is nothing to prove. Moreover, this highly moral argument can be turned around. If the voluntary martyrdom of the suicide bombers proves nothing, then the involuntary martyrdom of the victims of the attack proves nothing either, and there is something unseemly and obscene in making a moral argument out of it (this is in no way to deny their suffering and death).

Another argument in bad faith: these terrorists exchanged their deaths for a place in paradise; their act was not a disinterested one, hence it is not authentic; it would be disinterested only if they did not believe in God, if they saw no hope in death, as is the case with us (yet Christian martyrs assumed precisely such a sublime equivalence). There again, then, they are not fighting fair, since they get salvation, which we cannot even continue to hope for. So we mourn our deaths while they can turn theirs into very high-definition stakes.

Fundamentally, all this — causes, proof, truth, rewards, ends and means — is a typically Western form of calculation. We even evaluate death in terms of interest rates, in value-for-money terms. An economic calculation that is a poor man's calculation — poor men who no longer even have the courage to pay the price.

What can happen now — apart from war, which is itself merely a conventional safety shield [*écran de protection*]? There is talk of bio-terrorism, bacteriological warfare or nuclear terrorism. Yet that is no longer of the order of the symbolic challenge, but of annihilation pure and simple, with no element of risk or glory: it is of the order of the final solution. Now, it is a mistake to see terrorist action as obeying a purely destructive logic. It seems to me that the action of the terrorists, from which death is inseparable (this is precisely what makes it a symbolic act), does not seek the impersonal elimination of the other. Everything lies in the challenge and the duel — that is to say, everything still lies in a dual, personal relation with the opposing power. It is that power which humiliated you, so it too must be humiliated. And not merely exterminated. It has to be made to lose face. And you never achieve that by pure force and eliminating the other party: it must, rather, be targeted and wounded in a genuinely adversarial relation. Apart from the pact that binds the terrorists together, there is also something of a dual pact with the adversary. This is, then, precisely the opposite of the cowardice of which they stand accused, and it is precisely the opposite of what the Americans did in the Gulf War (and which they are currently beginning again in Afghanistan), where the target is invisible and is liquidated operationally.

In all these vicissitudes, what stays with us, above all else, is the sight of the images. This impact of the images, and their fascination, are necessarily what we retain, since images are, whether we like it or not, our primal scene. And, at the same time as they have radicalized the world situation, the events in New York can also be said to have radicalized the relation of the image to reality. Whereas we were dealing before with an uninterrupted profusion of banal images and a seamless flow of sham events, the terrorist act in New York has resuscitated both images and events.

Among the other weapons of the system which they turned round against it, the terrorists exploited the 'real time' of images, their instantaneous worldwide transmission, just as they exploited stock-market speculation, electronic information and air traffic. The role of images is highly ambiguous. For, at the same time as they exalt the event, they also take it hostage. They serve to multiply it to infinity and, at the same time, they are a diversion and a neutralization (this was already the case with the events of 1968). The image consumes the event, in the sense that it absorbs it and offers it for consumption. Admittedly, it gives it unprecedented impact, but impact as image-event.

How do things stand with the real event, then,

if reality is everywhere infiltrated by images, virtuality and fiction? In the present case, we thought we had seen (perhaps with a certain relief) a resurgence of the real, and of the violence of the real, in an allegedly virtual universe. 'There's an end to all your talk about the virtual – this is something real!' Similarly, it was possible to see this as a resurrection of history beyond its proclaimed end. But does reality actually outstrip fiction? If it seems to do so, this is because it has absorbed fiction's energy, and has itself become fiction. We might almost say that reality is jealous of fiction, that the real is jealous of the image. . . . It is a kind of duel between them, a contest to see which can be the most unimaginable.

The collapse of the World Trade Center towers is unimaginable, but that is not enough to make it a real event. An excess of violence is not enough to open on to reality. For reality is a principle, and it is this principle that is lost. Reality and fiction are inextricable, and the fascination with the attack is primarily a fascination with the image (both its exultatory and its catastrophic consequences are themselves largely imaginary).

In this case, then, the real is superadded to the image like a bonus of terror, like an additional *frisson*: not only is it terrifying, but, what is more, it is real. Rather than the violence of the real being there first, and the *frisson* of the image being added to it, the image is there first, and the *frisson* of the real is added. Something like an additional fiction, a fiction surpassing fiction. Ballard (after Borges) talked like this of reinventing the real as the ultimate and most redoubtable fiction.

The terrorist violence here is not, then, a blowback of reality, any more than it is a blowback of history. It is not 'real'. In a sense, it is worse: it is symbolic. Violence in itself may be perfectly banal and inoffensive. Only symbolic violence is generative of singularity. And in this singular event, in this Manhattan disaster movie, the twentieth century's two elements of mass fascination are combined: the white magic of the cinema and the black magic of terrorism; the white light of the image and the black light of terrorism.

We try retrospectively to impose some kind of meaning on it, to find some kind of interpretation. But there is none. And it is the radicality of the spectacle, the brutality of the spectacle, which alone is original and irreducible. The spectacle of terrorism forces the terrorism of spectacle upon us. And, against this immoral fascination (even if it unleashes a universal moral reaction), the political order can do nothing. This is *our* theatre of cruelty, the only one we have left – extraordinary in that it unites the most extreme degree of the spectacular and the highest level of challenge. . . . It is at one and the same time the dazzling micro-model of a kernel of real violence with the maximum possible echo – hence the purest form of spectacle – and a sacrificial model mounting the purest symbolic form of defiance to the historical and political order.

We would forgive them any massacre if it had

a meaning, if it could be interpreted as historical violence – this is the moral axiom of good violence. We would pardon them any violence if it were not given media exposure ('terrorism would be nothing without the media'). But this is all illusion. There is no 'good' use of the media; the media are part of the event, they are part of the terror, and they work in both directions.

The repression of terrorism spirals around as unpredictably as the terrorist act itself. No one knows where it will stop, or what turnabouts there may yet be. There is no possible distinction, at the level of images and information, between the spectacular and the symbolic, no possible distinction between the 'crime' and the crackdown. And it is this uncontrollable unleashing of reversibility that is terrorism's true victory. A victory that is visible in the subterranean ramifications and infiltrations of the event – not just in the direct economic, political, financial slump in the whole of the system – and the resulting moral and psychological downturn –

but in the slump in the value-system, in the whole ideology of freedom, of free circulation, and so on, on which the Western world prided itself, and on which it drew to exert its hold over the rest of the world.

To the point that the idea of freedom, a new and recent idea, is already fading from minds and mores, and liberal globalization is coming about in precisely the opposite form – a police-state globalization, a total control, a terror based on 'law-and-order' measures. Deregulation ends up in a maximum of constraints and restrictions, akin to those of a fundamentalist society.

A fall-off in production, consumption, speculation and growth (but certainly not in corruption!): it is as though the global system were making a strategic fallback, carrying out a painful revision of its values – in defensive reaction, as it would seem, to the impact of terrorism, but responding, deep down, to its secret injunctions: enforced regulation as a product of absolute disorder, but a regulation it imposes on itself – internalizing, as it were, its own defeat.

Another aspect of the terrorists' victory is that all other forms of violence and the destabilization of order work in its favour. Internet terrorism, biological terrorism, the terrorism of anthrax and rumour – all are ascribed to Bin Laden. He might even claim natural catastrophes as his own. All the forms of disorganization and perverse circulation operate to his advantage. The very structure of generalized world trade works in favour of impossible exchange. It is like an 'automatic writing' of terrorism, constantly refuelled by the involuntary terrorism of news and information. With all the panic consequences which ensue; if, in the current anthrax scare,* the hysteria spreads spontaneously by instantaneous crystallization, like a chemical solution at the mere contact of a molecule, this is because the whole system has reached a critical mass which makes it vulnerable to any aggression.

---

* This text was written in October 2001 and published in *Le Monde* on November 3 2001.

There is no remedy for this extreme situation, and war is certainly not a solution, since it merely offers a rehash of the past, with the same deluge of military forces, bogus information, senseless bombardment, emotive and deceitful language, technological deployment and brainwashing. Like the Gulf War: a non-event, an event that does not really take place.

And this indeed is its *raison-d'être*: to substitute, for a real and formidable, unique and unforeseeable event, a repetitive, rehashed pseudo-event. The terrorist attack corresponded to a precedence of the event over all interpretative models; whereas this mindlessly military, technological war corresponds, conversely, to the model's precedence over the event, and hence to a conflict over phoney stakes, to a situation of 'no contest'. War as continuation of the absence of politics by other means.

REQUIEM FOR THE
TWIN TOWERS

A version of this paper was Baudrillard's contribution to a debate on the events of September 11 2001, the 'Rencontres philosophiques outre-Atlantique', organized jointly by New York University and France Culture in Washington Square, Manhattan. The formal contributions were broadcast on France Culture on the afternoon of February 23 2002. The debate, which was largely conducted in French, was chaired by Tom Bishop; other participants were Jacques Rancière, Charles Larmore and Mark Lilla. The footnotes, which refer to slight variations between the written text and the version delivered in New York, are my own [Trans.].

The September 11 attacks also concern architecture, since what was destroyed was one of the most prestigious of buildings, together with a whole (Western) value-system and a world order.[1]

1   In the New York debate, Baudrillard prefaced his talk with the following comments: 'There is an absolute difficulty in speaking of an absolute event. That is to say, in providing an analysis of it that is not an explanation – as I don't think there is any possible explanation of this event, either by intellectuals or by others – but its *analogon*, so to speak; an analysis which might possibly be as unacceptable as the event, but strikes the . . . let us say, symbolic imagination in more or less the same way.'

It may, then, be useful to begin with a historical and architectural analysis of the Twin Towers, in order to grasp the symbolic significance of their destruction.

First of all, why the *Twin* Towers? Why *two* towers at the World Trade Center?

All Manhattan's tall buildings had been content to confront each other in a competitive verticality, and the product of this was an architectural panorama reflecting the capitalist system itself – a pyramidal jungle, whose famous image stretched out before you as you arrived from the sea. That image changed after 1973, with the building of the World Trade Center. The effigy of the system was no longer the obelisk and the pyramid, but the punch card and the statistical graph. This architectural graphism is the embodiment of a system that is no longer competitive, but digital and countable, and from which competition has disappeared in favour of networks and monopoly.

Perfect parallelepipeds, standing over 1,300 feet tall, on a square base. Perfectly balanced, blind communicating vessels (they say terrorism is 'blind', but the towers were blind too – monoliths no longer opening on to the outside world, but subject to artificial conditioning[2]). The fact that there were two of them signifies the end of any original reference. If there had been only one, monopoly would not have been perfectly embodied. Only the doubling of the sign truly puts an end to what it designates.

There is a particular fascination in this redu-plication. However tall they may have been, the

---

2 In New York, Baudrillard here glossed: 'Air condition-ing, but mental conditioning too'.

two towers signified, none the less, a halt to verticality. They were not of the same breed as the other buildings. They culminated in the exact reflection of each other. The glass and steel façades of the Rockefeller Center buildings still mirrored each other in an endless specularity. But the Twin Towers no longer had any façades, any faces. With the rhetoric of verticality disappears also the rhetoric of the mirror. There remains only a kind of black box, a series closed on the figure two, as though architecture, like the system, was now merely a product of cloning, and of a changeless genetic code.

New York is the only city in the world that has, throughout its history, tracked the present form of the system and all its many developments with such prodigious fidelity. We must, then, assume that the collapse of the towers – itself a unique event in the history of modern cities – prefigures a kind of dramatic ending and, all in all, disappearance both of this form of architecture and of the world system it embodies. Shaped in the pure computer image of banking and finance, (ac)countable and digital, they were in a sense its brain, and in striking there the terrorists have struck at the brain, at the nerve-centre of the system.

The violence of globalization also involves architecture, and hence the violent protest against it also involves the destruction of that architecture. In terms of collective drama, we can say that the horror for the 4,000 victims of dying in those towers was inseparable from the horror of living in them – the horror of living and working in sarcophagi of concrete and steel.

These architectural monsters, like the Beaubourg Centre, have always exerted an ambiguous fascination, as have the extreme forms of modern technology in general – a contradictory feeling

of attraction and repulsion, and hence, somewhere, a secret desire to see them disappear. In the
case of the Twin Towers, something particular is
added: precisely their symmetry and their
twin-ness. There is, admittedly, in this cloning and
perfect symmetry an aesthetic quality, a kind of
perfect crime against form, a tautology of form
which can give rise, in a violent reaction, to the
temptation to break that symmetry, to restore an
asymmetry, and hence a singularity.

Their destruction itself respected the symmetry of the towers: a double attack, separated by a
few minutes' interval, with a sense of suspense
between the two impacts. After the first, one
could still believe it was an accident. Only the second impact confirmed the terrorist attack. And in
the Queens air crash a month later, the TV sta-
tions waited, staying with the story (in France) for
four hours, waiting to broadcast a possible second
crash 'live'. Since that did not occur, we shall

never know now whether it was an accident or a terrorist act.

The collapse of the towers is the major symbolic event. Imagine they had not collapsed, or only one had collapsed: the effect would not have been the same at all. The fragility of global power would not have been so strikingly proven. The towers, which were the emblem of that power, still embody it in their dramatic end, which resembles a suicide. Seeing them collapse themselves, as if by implosion, one had the impression that they were committing suicide in response to the suicide of the suicide planes.

Were the Twin Towers destroyed, or did they collapse? Let us be clear about this: the two towers are both a physical, architectural object and a symbolic object[3] (symbolic of financial power and

3 In New York, Baudrillard added: 'symbolic in the weak sense, but symbolic, for all that'.

global economic liberalism). The architectural object was destroyed, but it was the symbolic object which was targeted and which it was intended to demolish. One might think the physical destruction brought about the symbolic collapse. But in fact no one, not even the terrorists, had reckoned on the total destruction of the towers. It was, in fact, their symbolic collapse that brought about their physical collapse, not the other way around.

As if the power bearing these towers suddenly lost all energy, all resilience; as though that arrogant power suddenly gave way under the pressure of too intense an effort: the effort always to be the unique world model.

So the towers, tired of being a symbol which was too heavy a burden to bear, collapsed, this time physically, in their totality. Their nerves of steel cracked. They collapsed vertically, drained of their strength, with the whole world looking on in astonishment.

The symbolic collapse came about, then, by a kind of unpredictable complicity – as though the entire system, by its internal fragility, joined in the game of its own liquidation, and hence joined in the game of terrorism. Very logically, and inexorably, the increase in the power of power heightens the will to destroy it. But there is more: somewhere, it was party to its own destruction. The countless disaster movies bear witness to this fantasy, which they attempt to exorcize with images and special effects. But the fascination they exert is a sign that acting-out is never very far away – the rejection of any system, including internal rejection, growing all the stronger as it approaches perfection or omnipotence. It has been said that 'Even God cannot declare war on Himself.' Well, He can. The West, in the position of God (divine omnipotence and absolute moral legitimacy), has become suicidal, and declared war on itself.

Even in their failure, the terrorists succeeded beyond their wildest hopes: in bungling their attack on the White House (while succeeding far beyond their objectives on the towers), they demonstrated unintentionally that that was not the essential target, that political power no longer means much, and real power lies elsewhere. As for what should be built in place of the towers, the problem is insoluble. Quite simply because one can imagine nothing equivalent that would be worth destroying – that would be worthy of being destroyed. The Twin Towers were worth destroying. One cannot say the same of many architectural works. Most things are not even worth destroying or sacrificing. Only works of prestige deserve that fate, for it is an honour. This proposition is not as paradoxical as it sounds, and it raises a basic issue for architecture: one should build only those things which, by their excellence, are worthy of being destroyed. Take a look around with this radical proposition in mind, and you will see what a pass we have come to. Not much would withstand this extreme hypothesis.

This brings us back to what should be the basic question for architecture, which architects never formulate: is it normal to build and construct? In fact it is not, and we should preserve the absolutely problematical character of the undertaking. Undoubtedly, the task of architecture — of good architecture — is to efface itself, to disappear as such. The towers, for their part, have disappeared. But they have left us the symbol of their disappearance, their disappearance as symbol. They, which were the symbol of omnipotence, have become, by their absence, the symbol of the possible disappearance of that omnipotence — which is perhaps an even more potent symbol.

Whatever becomes of that global omnipotence, it will have been destroyed here for a moment.

Moreover, although the two towers have disappeared, they have not been annihilated. Even in their pulverized state, they have left behind an intense awareness of their presence. No one who knew them can cease imagining them and the imprint they made on the skyline from all points of the city. Their end in material space has borne them off into a definitive imaginary space. By the grace of terrorism, the World Trade Center has become the world's most beautiful building – the eighth wonder of the world![4]

---

4 After delivering a slightly modified version of this last paragraph in New York, Baudrillard closed with the comment: 'So I set out to produce a Requiem, but it was also, in a way, a Te Deum.'

HYPOTHESES ON TERRORISM

We may dismiss from the outset the hypothesis that September 11 constituted merely an accident or incident on the path to irreversible globalization. An ultimately despairing hypothesis, since something very extraordinary occurred there, and to deny it is to admit that henceforth nothing can ever constitute an event, that we are doomed to play out the flawless logic of a global power capable of absorbing any resistance, any antagonism, and even strengthening itself by so doing – the terrorist act merely hastening the planetary ascendancy of a single power and a single way of thinking.

Counterposed to this zero hypothesis is the maximal one, the maximal gamble on the character of September 11 as event – event being defined here as that which, in a system of generalized exchange, suddenly creates a zone of impossible exchange: the impossible exchange of death at the heart of the event itself, and the impossible exchange of that event for any discourse whatever. Hence its symbolic potency, and it is this symbolic potency which struck us all in the Manhattan events.

According to the zero hypothesis, the terrorist event is insignificant. It ought not to have existed and, basically, it does not exist. This is to see things in terms of the idea that Evil is mere illusion or an accidental vicissitude in the trajectory of Good – in this case, the trajectory of the World Order and a happy Globalization. Theology has always based itself on this unreality of Evil as such.

Another hypothesis: it was an act of suicidal madmen, psychopaths, fanatics of a perverted cause, themselves manipulated by some evil power, which is merely exploiting the resentment and hatred of oppressed peoples to sate its destructive rage. The same hypothesis – but more favourably put, and attempting to lend terrorism a kind of historical rationale – is the one that sees it as the real expression of the despair of oppressed peoples. But this argument is itself suspect, since it condemns terrorism to represent global misery only in a definitive gesture of impotence. And even if it is granted that terrorism is a specific form of political contestation of the global order, this is generally done only to denounce its failure and, at the same time, its unintended effect, which is involuntarily to consolidate that order. This is the version advanced by Arundhati Roy who, while denouncing hegemonic power, denounces terrorism as its twin – the diabolical twin of the system. A small step, then, to imagine that if terrorism did not exist, the system would have invented it. And why not, then, see the September 11 attacks as a CIA stunt?

Here again, this is to suppose that all oppositional violence is ultimately complicit with the existing order. It is to disqualify the intentions of the actors, and the very stakes of their action. It is to reduce that action to its 'objective' consequences (the geopolitical consequences of September 11), and never to see it in terms of its own potency. And, anyway, who is manipulating whom? Who is playing the other's game? In this case, it is just as much the terrorists who profit by the advance of the system, in order themselves to gain power, in a race along parallel tracks in which the two opponents, contrary to what happened in class conflict and historical warfare, never actually meet.

We should go even further: rather than the hypothesis of an 'objective' complicity between terrorism and the world order, we should advance the exactly opposite hypothesis of a deep internal complicity between that power and the power ranged against it from the outside; of an internal instability and weakness which, in a sense, meet the violent destabilization of the terrorist act halfway. Without the hypothesis of this secret coalition, this collusive predisposition, one can understand nothing of terrorism and the impossibility of overcoming it.

If the aim of terrorism is to destabilize the global order merely by its own strength, in a head-on clash, then it is absurd: the relation of forces is so unequal and, in any case, that global order is already the site of such disorder and deregulation that there is no point whatever in adding to it. One even runs the risk, by this additional disorder, of reinforcing the police and security control systems, as we see on all sides today.

But perhaps that is the terrorists' dream: the dream of an immortal enemy. For, if the enemy no longer exists, it becomes difficult to destroy it. A tautology, admittedly, but terrorism is tautological, and its conclusion is a paradoxical syllogism: if the State really existed, it would give a political meaning to terrorism. Since terrorism manifestly has none (though it has other meanings), this is proof that the State does not exist, and that its power is derisory.

What, then, is the terrorists' secret message? In a Nasreddin story, we see him crossing the frontier each day with mules laden with sacks. Each time, the sacks are searched, but nothing is found. And Nasreddin continues to cross the frontier with his mules. Long afterwards, they ask him what in fact it was he was smuggling. And Nasreddin replies: 'I was smuggling mules.'

In this same way, we may wonder what it is that is really being smuggled here, behind all the apparent motives for the terrorist act – religion, martyrdom, vengeance or strategy? It is quite simply, through what seems to us like a suicide, the impossible exchange of death, the challenge to the system by the symbolic gift of death, which becomes an absolute weapon (the Towers seem to have understood this, since they responded with their own collapse).

This is the sovereign hypothesis: terrorism ultimately has no meaning, no objective, and cannot be measured by its 'real' political and historical consequences. And it is, paradoxically, because it has no meaning that it constitutes an event in a world increasingly saturated with meaning and efficacy.

The sovereign hypothesis is the one that conceives of terrorism, beyond its spectacular violence, beyond Islam and America, as the emergence of a radical antagonism at the very heart of the process of globalization, of a force irreducible to this integral technical and mental realization of the world, irreducible to this inexorable movement towards a completed global order.

A vital counterforce grappling with the death force of the system. A force of defiance to a global-ity totally soluble in circulation or exchange. A force of an irreducible singularity, the more violent as the system extends its hegemony – up to a rup-tural event like that of September 11, which does not resolve this antagonism, but lends it, at a stroke, a symbolic dimension.

Terrorism invents nothing, inaugurates noth-ing. It simply carries things to the extreme, to the point of paroxysm. It exacerbates a certain state of things, a certain logic of violence and uncertainty. The system itself, by the speculative extension of all exchange, the random and virtual form it imposes everywhere – lean production, floating capital, forced mobility and acceleration – causes a general principle of uncertainty to prevail, which terrorism simply translates into total insecurity. Terrorism is unreal and unrealistic? But our virtual reality, our systems of information and communication, have themselves too, and for a long time, been beyond the reality principle. As for terror, we know it is already present everywhere, in institutional violence, both mental and physical, in homeopathic doses. Terrorism merely crystallizes all the ingredients in suspension. It puts the finishing touches to the orgy of power, liberation, flows and calculation which the Twin Towers embodied, while being the violent deconstruction of that extreme form of efficiency and hegemony.

So, at Ground Zero, in the rubble of global power, we can only, despairingly, find our own image.

There isn't, in fact, anything else to see at Ground Zero – not even a sign of hostility towards an invisible enemy. What prevails there is merely the American people's immense compassion for itself – with star-spangled banners, commemorative messages, the cult of victims and of those postmodern heroes, the firefighters and the police. Compassion as the national passion of a people that wants to be alone with God, and prefers to see itself struck down by God than by some evil power. 'God bless America' has become: 'At last, God has struck us.' Consternation, but ultimately eternal gratitude for this divine solicitude that has made us victims.

The reasoning of moral consciousness is as follows: since we are the Good, it can only be Evil that has struck us. But if, for those who see themselves as the incarnation of Good, Evil is unimaginable, it can only be God who strikes them. And to punish them for what, ultimately, if not for an excess of Virtue and Power, for the excess signified by the non-division of Good and Power? A punishment for having gone too far in the Good and the incarnation of the Good. Which does not displease them, and will not prevent them from continuing to do Good without the slightest misgivings. And hence finding themselves even more alone with God. And hence being even more profoundly unaware of the existence of Evil.

The twin sister of compassion (as much a twin as the two towers) is arrogance. You weep over your own misfortune, and at the same time you are the best. And what gives us the right to be the best is that from now on, we are victims. This is the perfect alibi; it is the whole mental hygiene of the victim, through which all guilt is resolved, and which allows one to use misfortune as though it were, so to speak, a credit card.

The Americans lacked such a wound (at Pearl Harbor they suffered an act of war, not a symbolic attack). An ideal reverse of fortune for a nation at last wounded at its heart and free, having atoned for it, to exert its power in all good conscience. A situation science fiction dreamed of from the beginning: that of some obscure force that would wipe them out and which, until that point, merely existed in their unconscious (or some other recess of their minds). And all of a sudden, it materializes through the good grace of terrorism! The axis of Evil takes hold of America's unconscious, and realizes by violence what was merely a fantasy and a dream thought!

It all comes from the fact that the Other, like Evil, is unimaginable. It all comes from the impossibility of conceiving of the Other – friend or enemy – in its radical otherness, in its irreconcilable foreignness. A refusal rooted in the total identification with oneself around moral values and technical power. That is the America that takes itself for America and which, bereft of otherness, eyes itself with the wildest compassion.

Let us be clear: America is here merely the allegory or universal figure of any power incapable of bearing the spectre of opposition. How can the Other, unless he is an idiot, a psychopath or a crank, want to be different, irremediably different, without even a desire to sign up to our universal gospel?

Such is the arrogance of Empire – as in Borges's allegory (the mirror people[1]), where the defeated peoples are exiled into the mirrors, from where they are condemned to reflect the image of the conquerors. (But one day they begin to look less and less like their conquerors, and in the end they smash the mirrors and attack the Empire once again).

There is this same exile into the mirror of resemblance in Philippe Muray's address to the *Dear*

1 In 'Fauna of Mirrors', *The Book of Imaginary Beings* (Harmondsworth: Penguin, 1974), pp. 67–8 [Trans.].

Jihadists:[2] 'We produced you, jihadists and terrorists, and you will end up prisoners of resemblance.
Your radicalism is something we passed on to you.
We can do this because we are indifferent to everything, including our own values. You cannot kill us
because we are already dead. You think you are
fighting us, but you are unconsciously on our side.
You are already assimilated.' Or, elsewhere: 'You
have worked well, but you have merely killed your-
selves off as a singular force . . . . By your very act,
you have re-entered the global game you execrate.'

A statement of the abject nature of our dying
culture, but also a statement of the failure of any
violence antagonistic to it, or believing itself to be
so. Poor rebels, poor innocents! 'We shall defeat
you because we are deader than you!' *But it is not the*

2   Philippe Muray, *Chers djihadistes* (Paris: Mille et une nuits,
    2002) [Trans.].

same death that is at issue. When Western culture sees all its values extinguished one by one, it turns inward on itself in the very worst way. Our death is an extinction, an annihilation; it is not a symbolic stake. Herein lies our poverty. When a singularity throws its own death into the ring, it escapes this slow extermination, it dies its own natural death. This is an immense game of double or quits. In committing suicide, the singularity suicides the other at the same time – we might say that the terrorist acts literally 'suicided' the West. A death for a death, then, but transfigured by the symbolic stakes. 'We have already devastated our world, what more do you want?' says Muray. But precisely, *we have merely devastated this world, it still has to be destroyed.* Destroyed symbolically. This is not at all the same undertaking. And though we did the first part, only others are going to be able to do the second.

Even in vengeance and warfare, we can see the same lack of imagination – the same inability to regard the other as a fully fledged adversary, the same magical solution, which is to exterminate him and obliterate him unceremoniously.

To make Islam the embodiment of Evil would be to do it honour (and to do oneself honour in the process). But we don't see things that way: when it is said that Islam is Evil, the implication is that it *is not well*, that it is sick, and that it is violent because it is sick, because it sees itself as a humiliated victim, and is nursing its resentment instead of taking its place joyously in the New World Order. Islam is regressive and fundamentalist out of despair. But if it becomes offensive, then it must be reduced to impotence. In a word, Islam is not what it ought to be. And what, then, of the West?

There is the same inability to contemplate for one moment that these 'fanatics' might commit themselves entirely 'freely', without in any way being blind, mad or manipulated. For we have the monopoly of the evaluation of Good and Evil, the implication being that the only 'free and responsible' choice cannot but be in keeping with our moral law. Which means imputing any resistance to, any violation of, our values to a blinding of consciousness (but where does this blinding come from?). That the 'free and enlightened' man should necessarily choose Good is our universal prejudice – and a paradoxical one it is too, since the man who has this 'rational' choice allotted to him is no longer, ultimately, free to decide (psychoanalysis, too, has specialized in the interpretation of these 'resistances').

On this point, Lichtenberg tells us something stranger and more original – namely, that the proper use of freedom is to abuse it, and make excessive use of it. And this includes taking responsibility for one's own death and that of others.

Hence the absurdity of the epithet 'cowardly' that is applied to the terrorists: cowardly for having chosen suicide, cowardly for having sacrificed the innocent (when we don't accuse *them* of taking advantage of this to reach paradise).

All the same, we should try to get beyond the moral imperative of unconditional respect for human life, and conceive that one might respect, both in the other and in oneself, something other than, and more than, life (existence isn't everything, it is even the least of things): a destiny, a cause, a form of pride or of sacrifice. There are symbolic stakes which far exceed existence and freedom – which we find it unbearable to lose, because we have made them the fetishistic values of a universal humanist order. So we cannot imagine a terrorist act committed with entire autonomy and 'freedom of conscience'. Now, choice in terms of symbolic obligations is sometimes profoundly mysterious – as in the case of Romand, the man with the double life, who murdered his whole family, not for fear of being unmasked, but for fear of inflicting on them the profound disappointment of discovering his deception.[3] Committing suicide would not have expunged the crime from the record; he would merely have passed the shame off on to the others. Where is the courage, where the cowardice? The question of freedom, one's own or that of others, no longer poses itself in terms of moral consciousness, and a higher freedom must allow us to dispose of it to the point of abusing or sacrificing it. Omar Khayyam: 'Rather one freeman bind with chains of love than set a thousand prisoned captives free.'

Seen in that light, this is almost an overturning of the dialectic of domination, a paradoxical

---

3   See Emmanuel Carrère, *The Adversary: A True Story of Murder and Deception*, trans. Linda Coverdale (London: Bloomsbury, 2001) [Trans.].

inversion of the master–slave relationship. In the past, the master was the one who was exposed to death, and could gamble with it. The slave was the one deprived of death and destiny, the one doomed to survival and labour. How do things stand today? We, the powerful, sheltered now from death and overprotected on all sides, occupy exactly the position of the slave; whereas those whose deaths are at their own disposal, and who do not have survival as their exclusive aim, are the ones who today symbolically occupy the position of master.

Another serious objection – no longer this time with regard to motives, but to the symbolic tenor of the terrorist act. Are we dealing, in the September 11 attack – in this violent challenge to the triumphant logic of globalization – with a symbolic act in the strong sense (that is to say, implying a turnaround and transmutation of values)? According to Caroline Heinrich, for example, the terrorists, in attacking a logic of simulation and indifference in the name of a system of values and higher reality, can be said merely to have revived a new identitary logic. 'Against the logic of indifference,' she says, 'the terrorists are trying to restore a meaning to something that no longer has any.' The Real for us being what it is – that is to say, a referential illusion – the terrorists could merely be said to be substituting for it new stakes and new values dredged up from the ancient past.

Something for which Philippe Muray also criticizes them: 'We had liquidated all our values; that was indeed the sense of our whole history, and you bring us back your phantom values, your phantom identity, your "integrity", which you set against a disintegrated world.' The terrorists are taking 'simulation' referents (the towers, the market, the Western mega-culture) for real ones. Against the inhumanity of integral exchange, they are once again inaugurating a metaphysics of truth (following

Caroline Heinrich here still). Now, the point is not to take it out on simulation, but *to take it out on the truth itself*. There is no point attacking simulacra, if it means falling back into truth. There is no point attacking the virtual, if it means falling back into reality.

All the more so, according to Caroline Heinrich, as the terrorists are themselves in out-and-out simulation: the terrorist act is generated by models. It is, even, a remarkable example of the precedence of models over the Real (Hollywood directors have been called in as consultants by antiterrorist strategists). Moreover, their action is modelled in every respect on the technological devices of the system. How can one, then, by playing the same game as the system, claim to overturn its goals?

The objection is a strong one, but reductive in so far as it confines itself to the religious and fundamentalist discourse of the terrorists, by which they claim effectively to contest the global system in the name of a higher truth. Yet it is not in discourse, but in the act itself that the 'minimal irruption of reversibility' which makes it a symbolic act resides. The terrorists are making an attack upon a system of integral reality by an act which has, in the very moment of its perpetration, neither true meaning nor reference in another world. The aim is simply to wreck the system — itself indifferent to its own values — by means of its own weapons. Even more than the system's technological weapons, the key arm they appropriate, and turn to decisive effect, is the non-meaning and indifference which are at the heart of the system.

A strategy of turning around and overturning power, not in the name of a moral or religious confrontation, nor some 'clash of civilizations', but as a result of the pure and simple unacceptability of that global power.

There is, moreover, no need to be an Islamist, or to appeal to a higher truth, to find this global order unacceptable. Islamist or not, we share this fundamental rejection, and there are many signs of fracture and disarray – of fragility – at the heart of this power itself. This is the 'truth' of the terrorist act. There is no other, and certainly not the truth of a fundamentalism to which it is referred, merely the better to disqualify it.

What terrorism revives is something that cannot be traded in a system of differences and generalized exchange. Difference and indifference can perfectly well be traded for one another. What constitutes an event is that for which there is no equivalent. And there is no equivalent for the terrorist act in some transcendent truth.

When Caroline Heinrich counterposes graffiti to terrorism as the only rigorous symbolic act, in so far as graffiti signifies nothing and makes use of empty signs to reduce them to absurdity, she does not realize how right she is. Graffiti is indeed a terrorist act (itself also with New York as its place of origin), not by its identity claim – 'I am so-and-so, I exist, I live in New York' – but by its disinscription of the walls and architecture of the city, by the violent deconstruction of the signifier itself (the graffiti-tattooed subway trains plunged right into the heart of New York in exactly the same way as the terrorists hurtled their Boeings into the Twin Towers).

The question is that of the Real. According to Žižek, the passion of the twentieth and twenty-first centuries is the eschatological passion for the Real, the nostalgic passion for that lost or disappearing object.[4] And the terrorists might be said, ultimately,

---

4   See Slavoj Žižek, *Welcome to the Desert of the Real!* (London and New York: Verso, 2002), p. 5. (Though it should be pointed out that Baudrillard had not seen this work at the

merely to be responding to this pathetic demand
for reality.

For Philippe Muray, too, the jihadists' terrorism is merely the last stirring of a dying reality –
the aftermath of a dramatic history that is now
coming to an end, and is paralysed precisely
because it is moribund. But this calling to order of
the Real and History is itself a thing of pathos, as
it corresponds to an earlier phase, and not to the
present integral-reality phase which is that of
globalization. At this stage, no negativity whatever can provide a response. To this 'integrist'
offensive of the global system, the only response
can come through the irruption of a singularity,

time of writing, but had had access only to a much shorter
conference paper by Žižek. The phrase 'the passion for
the Real' in Žižek's text is taken, with acknowledgement,
from an as yet unpublished work by Alain Badiou, entitled
Le Siècle [Trans.].

which, for its part, has nothing to do with the Real.

The most recent of the versions of September 11, and the most eccentric, is that it was all the product of an internal terrorist plot (CIA, fundamentalist extreme right, etc.). A thesis that appeared when doubt was cast on the air attack on the Pentagon and, by extension, the attack on the Twin Towers (in Thierry Meyssan's *9/11: The Big Lie*).

And what if it was all untrue? If it was all faked up? A thesis so unreal that it deserves to be taken into account, just as every exceptional event deserves to be doubted: we always have in us a demand both for a radical event and for a total deception. A phantasy of foul machination which does indeed, quite often, turn out to be true: we have lost count of the murderous acts of provocation, the attacks and 'accidents' staged by all kinds of secret groups and services.

Above and beyond the truth of the matter, of which we shall perhaps never have any knowledge, what remains of this thesis is, once again, that the dominant power is the instigator of everything, including effects of subversion and violence, which are of the order of *trompe-l'œil*. The worst of this is that it is again we who perpetrated it. This, admittedly, brings no great glory on our democratic values, but it is still better than conceding to obscure jihadists the power to inflict such a defeat on us. Already with the Lockerbie Boeing crash, the theory of technical failure was for a long time preferred to that of a terrorist act. Even if it is a serious matter to admit one's own shortcomings, it is still preferable to admitting the other party's power (which does not exclude the paranoid denunciation of the axis of Evil).

If it were to turn out that such a mystification were possible, if the event were entirely faked up, then clearly it would no longer have any symbolic significance (if the Twin Towers were blown up from the inside – the crash not being sufficient to make them collapse – it would be very difficult to say they had committed suicide!). This would merely be a political conspiracy. And yet . . . . Even if all this were the doing of some clique of extremists or military men, it would still be the sign (as in the Oklahoma bombing) of a self-destructive internal violence, of a society's obscure predisposition to contribute to its own doom – as illustrated by the high-level dissensions between the CIA and FBI which, by reciprocally neutralizing information, gave the terrorists the unprecedented chance to succeed.

September 11 will have raised with some violence the question of reality, of which the fanciful conspiracy theory is the imaginary by-product. Hence, perhaps, the vehemence with which this theory has been rejected on all sides. Is it because it may be seen as anti-American, and absolves the terrorists from blame? (But to absolve them from blame is to relieve them of responsibility for the event, which comes back round again to the contemptuous view that the Islamists would never have been capable of such a feat.) No, it is, rather, the 'denial' aspect of this theory that explains the violence of the reaction. The denial of reality is terroristic in itself. Anything is better than to contest reality as such. What has to be saved is, above all, the reality principle. 'Negationism' is public enemy number one.[5] Now, in fact, we already live largely in a negationist society. No event is 'real' any longer. Terror attacks, trials, wars, corruption, opinion polls – there's nothing now that isn't rigged or undecidable. Government, the authorities and institutions

5   The French term 'négationnisme' usually designates what in English is called 'Holocaust denial', though clearly a wider sense is intended here [Trans.].

are the first victims of this fall from grace of the principles of truth and reality. Incredulity rages. The conspiracy theory merely adds a somewhat burlesque episode to this situation of mental desta-bilization. Hence the urgent need to combat this creeping negationism and, at all costs, safeguard a reality that is now kept alive on a drip. For though we can range a great machinery of repression and deterrence against physical insecurity and terror-ism, nothing will protect us from this mental insecurity.

Moreover, all the security strategies are merely extensions of terror. And it is the real victory of ter-rorism that it has plunged the whole of the West into the obsession with security – that is to say, into a veiled form of perpetual terror.

The spectre of terrorism is forcing the West to terrorize itself – the planetary police network being the equivalent of the tension of a universal Cold

War, of a fourth world war imprinting itself upon bodies and mores.

Thus, for example, the world's leaders met recently in Rome to sign a treaty which, they all proclaim, puts a final end to the Cold War. But they didn't even leave the airport. They stayed on the tarmac, surrounded by armoured cars, barbed wire and helicopters – that is to say, by all the symbols of the new Cold War, the war of armed security, of the perpetual deterrence of an invisible enemy.

Neither politically nor economically did the abolition of the Twin Towers put the global system in check. Something else is at issue here: the stunning impact of the attack, the insolence of its success and, as a result, the loss of credibility, the collapse of image. For the system can function only if it can exchange itself for its own image, reflect itself like the towers in their twinness, find its equivalent in an

ideal reference. It is this that makes it invulnera-
ble — and it is this equivalence that has been
smashed. It is in this sense that, while it is every bit
as elusive as terrorism, it has none the less been
struck in the heart.

THE VIOLENCE OF
THE GLOBAL

Current terrorism is not the descendant of a traditional history of anarchy, nihilism and fanaticism. It is contemporaneous with globalization and, in order to grasp its features, we should briefly go over a genealogy of that globalization, in its relation to the universal and the singular.

Between the terms 'global' and 'universal' there is a deceptive similarity. Universality is the universality of human rights, freedoms, culture and democracy. Globalization is the globalization of technologies, the market, tourism and information. Globalization seems irreversible, whereas the universal would seem, rather, to be on the way out. At least as it has constituted itself as a system of values on the scale of Western modernity, which has no equivalent in any other culture.

Any culture that universalizes loses its singularity and dies. This is how it is with all those we have destroyed by forcibly assimilating them, but it is also the case with our own culture in its pretension to universality. The difference is that the other cultures died of their singularity, which is a fine death, whereas we are dying of the loss of all singularity, of the extermination of all our values, which is an ignoble death.

We think the ideal destination of any value is its elevation to the universal, without gauging the lethal danger that promotion represents: much rather than an elevation, it is a dilution towards the zero degree of value. In the Enlightenment, universalization occurred by excess, in an ascending course of progress. Today it occurs by default, by a flight into the lowest common denominator. This is how it is with human rights, democracy and freedom: their expansion corresponds to their weakest definition.

In fact, the universal comes to grief in globalization. The globalization of trade puts an end to the universality of values. It is the triumph of single-track thinking over universal thought. What globalizes first is the market, the profusion of exchanges and of all products, the perpetual flow of money. Culturally, it is the promiscuity of all signs and all values or, in other words, pornography. For the global diffusion of anything and everything over the networks *is* pornography: no need for sexual obscenity, this interactive copulation is enough. At the end of this process, there is no longer any difference between the global and the universal. The universal itself is globalized; democracy and human rights circulate just like any other global product — like oil or capital.

What comes with the transition from the universal to the global is both a homogenization and a fragmentation to infinity. The central gives way not to the local, but to the dislocated. The concentric gives way not to the decentred, but to the eccentric. And discrimination and exclusion are not accidental consequences; they are part of the very logic of globalization.

We may wonder, then, whether the universal has not already succumbed to its own critical mass, and whether it and modernity have ever existed anywhere other than in discourse and official moralities. For us, at any rate, the mirror of the universal is shattered. But this is perhaps an opportunity, for in the fragments of this shattered mirror, all the singularities are resurfacing: those we believe to be threatened are surviving, while those we thought to be extinct are reviving.

The situation is becoming radicalized as universal values lose their authority and legitimacy. So long as they could assert themselves as mediating values, they succeeded, more or less well, in integrating singularities, as differences, into a universal culture of difference. But they can no longer do this now, as triumphant globalization has swept away all differences and all values, bringing into being an entirely in-different culture (or lack of it). Once the universal has disappeared, all that remains is the all-powerful global technostructure, set over against singularities that are now returned to the wild and left to themselves.

The universal has had its historical chance, but today, confronted on the one hand with a global order to which there is no alternative and, on the other, with singularities drifting off on their own or

rising up against the system, the concepts of freedom, democracy and human rights cut a very pale
figure, being merely the ghosts of a vanished universal.

The universal was a culture of transcendence, of
the subject and the concept, of the Real and repre-
sentation. The virtual space of the global is the
space of the screen and the network, of immanence
and the digital, of a dimensionless space–time. In
the universal, there was still a natural reference to
the world, to the body and to memory. A kind of
dialectical tension and critical movement which
found their form in historical and revolutionary violence. It is the expulsion of this critical negativity
which opens on to another kind of violence, the
violence of the global: the supremacy of positivity
alone and of technical efficiency, total organization,
integral circulation, the equivalence of all
exchanges. Hence the end of the role of the intel-
lectual, bound up with the Enlightenment and the

universal – and also the end of the activist, who was linked to contradictions and historical violence.

Is there some inevitability to globalization? All cultures but our own escaped, one way or another, the fated outcome of abstract exchange. Where is the critical threshold of transition to the universal, and then to the global? What is this dizzying whirl that drives the world to the abstraction of the Idea, and that other which drives it to the unconditional realization of the Idea?

For the universal was an Idea. When it realizes itself in the global, it commits suicide as Idea, as ideal end. Having become the sole reference – and a humanity immanent in itself having occupied the empty place of the dead God – the human now reigns alone, but it no longer has any ultimate rationale. No longer having any enemy, it generates one from within, and secretes all kinds of inhuman metastases.

Hence this violence of the global. The violence of a system that hounds out any form of negativity or singularity, including that ultimate form of singularity that is death itself. The violence of a society in which conflict is virtually banned and death forbidden. A violence which, in a sense, puts an end to violence itself, and works to set in place a world freed from any natural order, whether it be that of the body, sex, birth or death. More than violence, indeed, we should speak of virulence. This violence is viral: it operates by contagion, by chain reaction, and it gradually destroys all our immunities and our power to resist.

However, matters are not cut and dried, and globalization has not won the battle before it begins. In the face of this homogenizing, dissolving power, we see heterogeneous forces rising up everywhere – not merely different, but antagonistic. Behind the increasingly sharp resistance to globalization, social and political resistance, we should see more than mere archaic rejection: a kind of painful revisionism regarding the achievements of modernity and 'progress', a rejection not only of the global technostructure, but of the mental structure of equivalence of all cultures. This resurgence can assume aspects which, from the standpoint of enlightened thinking, seem violent, anomalous, irrational – ethnic, religious and linguistic collective forms, but also emotionally disturbed or neurotic individual forms. It would be a mistake to condemn these upsurges as populist, archaic, or even terroristic. Everything that constitutes an event today does so against this abstract universality – including Islam's antagonism to Western values (it is because it is the most vehement contestation of those values that it is enemy number one today).

Who can thwart the global system? Certainly not the anti-globalization movement, whose only objective is to curb deregulation. Its political impact may be considerable, but its symbolic impact is zero. That violence is still a kind of internal vicissitude which the system can surmount while retaining the upper hand.

What can thwart the system is not positive alternatives, but singularities. But these are neither positive nor negative. They are not an alternative; they are of another order. They do not conform to any value judgement, or obey any political reality principle. They can, as a consequence, be the best or the worst. They cannot be united in a general historical action. They thwart any dominant, single-track thinking, but they are not a single-track counter-thinking: they invent their own game and their own rules.

Singularities are not necessarily violent, and there are some subtle ones, such as those of language, art, the body or culture. But there are some violent ones, and terrorism is one of these. It is the one that avenges all the singular cultures that have paid with their disappearance for the establishment of this single global power.

It is not a question, then, of a 'clash of civilizations', but of an – almost anthropological – confrontation between an undifferentiated universal culture and everything which, in any field whatever, retains something of an irreducible alterity.

For global power, which is every bit as integrist as religious orthodoxy, all different, singular forms are heresies. On this account, they are doomed either to re-enter the global order, like it or not, or to disappear. The mission of the West (or, rather, of the former West, since for a long time now it has had no values of its own) is to subject the many different cultures, by any means available, to the unforgiving law of equivalence. A culture that has lost its values can only take its revenge on the values of others. Even wars – for example, the war in Afghanistan – aim initially, above and beyond political or economic strategies, to normalize savagery, to knock all territories into alignment. The objective is to quell any refractory zone, to colonize and tame all the wild spaces, whether in geographical space or in the realm of the mind.

The establishment of the global system is the product of a fierce jealousy: the jealous feelings of an in-different, low-definition culture towards high-definition cultures; of disenchanted, disintensified systems towards the cultures of high intensity; of desacralized societies towards sacrificial cultures or forms.

For such a system, any refractory form is virtually terroristic.[1] This is the case, again, with

---

1   It may even be argued that natural catastrophes are a form of terrorism. Large-scale technical accidents, such as the one at Chernobyl, have something of both the terrorist act

Afghanistan. That, on a particular territory, all 'democratic' freedoms and licence (music, television – even women's faces) can be prohibited, and that a country can stand out totally against what we call civilization (whatever the religious principle invoked) – these things are unbearable to the rest of the 'free' world. It is unacceptable for modernity to be rejected in its universal pretensions. That it

and the natural catastrophe about them. The poisoning by toxic gas in Bhopal in India – a technical accident – could have been a terrorist act. Any accidental air crash can be claimed by a terrorist group. The characteristic of irrational events is that they can be imputed to anyone or anything. At a pinch, anything can seem to the imagination to be of criminal origin: even a cold snap or an earthquake. And this is not new: during the Tokyo earthquake of 1923, thousands of Koreans, held responsible for the disaster, were massacred. In a system as integrated as our own, everything has the same destabilizing effect. Everything conspires towards the failure of a system that sees itself as infallible. And, in view of what we are already subjected to, within the framework of the system's rational, programmatic hold, we may wonder whether the worst catastrophe would not be the infallibility of the system itself.

should not appear as obvious Good, and the natural ideal of the human race; that the universality of our mores and values should be cast into doubt, if only in certain minds that are immediately characterized as fanatical – this is criminal so far as the consensual horizon and single-track thinking of the West are concerned.

This confrontation can be understood only in the light of symbolic obligation. To understand the rest of the world's hatred of the West, we have to over-turn all our usual ways of seeing. It is not the hatred of those from whom we have taken everything and given nothing back; it is the hatred of those to whom we have given everything without their being able to give it back. It is not, then, the hatred bred of deprivation and exploitation, but of humiliation. And it is to humiliation that the terrorism of September 11 was a response: one humiliation for another.

The worst thing for global power is not to be attacked or destroyed, but to be humiliated. And it was humiliated by September 11 because the terrorists inflicted something on it then that it cannot return. All the reprisals have merely been a system of physical retaliation, whereas that global power was defeated symbolically. War is a response to the aggression, but not to the challenge. The challenge can be taken up only by humiliating the other in return (but certainly not by bombing him to smithereens, or locking him up like a dog at Guantánamo).

The basis of all domination is the absence of reciprocation – we are still speaking here in terms of the fundamental rule. The unilateral gift is an act of power. And the Empire of Good, the violence of Good, lies precisely in giving without any possible reciprocation. This is to occupy the position of God. Or of the Master, who allows the slave to live in exchange for his labour (but labour is not a symbolic reciprocation, hence the only response is ultimately revolt and death). Even God left room for sacrifice. In the traditional order, there is still the possibility of giving something back to God, to nature, or to whatever it might be, in the form of sacrifice. This is what ensures the symbolic equilibrium between living beings and things. Today we no longer have anyone to whom we may give back, to whom we may repay the symbolic debt – and that is the curse of our culture. It is not that giving is impossible in this culture, but that the counter-gift is impossible, since all the paths of sacrifice have been neutralized and defused (there remains only a parody of sacrifice that can be seen in all the current forms of victimhood).

We are, as a result, in the relentless situation of receiving, always receiving. Not now from God or nature, but through a technical system of generalized exchange and general gratification. Everything is potentially given to us, and we are entitled to everything, like it or not. We are in the situation of slaves who have been allowed to live, and are bound by a debt that cannot be repaid. All this can function for a long time thanks to our insertion into relations of trade and the economic order but, at some point, the fundamental rule wins out. Then to this positive transference there inevitably comes a response in the form of a negative countertransference, a violent abreaction to this captive life, to this protected existence, to this saturation of existence. This reversion takes the form either of open violence (terrorism is part of this) or of the impotent denial characteristic of our modernity, of self-hatred and remorse – all negative passions that are the debased form of the impossible counter-gift.

What we detest in ourselves, the obscure object of our resentment, is this excess of reality, this excess of power and comfort, this universal availability, this definitive fulfilment – ultimately the fate the Grand Inquisitor reserves for the domesti-

cated masses in Dostoevsky. Now this is exactly
what the terrorists condemn in our culture – hence
the echo terrorism finds among us and the fascination it exerts.

As much as terrorism rests, then, on the despair
of the humiliated and insulted, it rests also on the
invisible despair of the privileged beneficiaries of globalization, on our own submission to an integral
technology, to a crushing virtual reality, to the grip of
networks and programmes, which perhaps represents
the involutive profile of the entire species, of the
human race become 'global' (doesn't the human race's
supremacy over the rest of the planet resemble the
West's supremacy over the rest of the world?). And
this invisible despair – our despair – is terminal, since
it arises out of the fulfilment of all desires.

If terrorism arises, in this way, out of this excess of
reality and its impossible exchange, out of this

profusion for which nothing is given in return and this forced resolution of conflicts, then the idea of extirpating it as an objective evil is a total illusion since, such as it is – in its absurdity and its meaninglessness – it is the verdict this society passes on itself, its self-condemnation.